Original title:
Bouquet of Ballads

Copyright © 2025 Creative Arts Management OÜ
All rights reserved.

Author: William Hawthorne
ISBN HARDBACK: 978-1-80566-611-0
ISBN PAPERBACK: 978-1-80566-896-1

A Symphony of Sunkissed Orchids

In a garden where giggles bloom,
Sunkissed orchids dance with a boom.
Their petals twirl in sunlit glee,
While bees beat drums, buzzing with spree.

The breeze brings whispers, soft and bright,
As flowers jest in pure delight.
They play peek-a-boo with the sun,
In this symphony, life's just begun!

Ballads Between Bloom and Wither

In the space where flowers laugh,
Bloom and wither share a gaffe.
One says, "I'm prettier than you!"
The other rolls eyes, "Oh, boo-hoo!"

With petals falling like confetti,
They argue over who is ready.
The sun chuckles, lighting their game,
"Both are lovely, just the same!"

The Language of Daffodil Dreams

Daffodils whisper secrets sweet,
Dreams on petals, oh what a treat!
They giggle and sway with the breeze,
"Hey there, tulips, come join with ease!"

Their tales of spring are quite absurd,
Of dancing ants and singing birds.
With every sway, they strike a pose,
In their garden, fun always grows!

Chords of the Crimson Rose

In the garden of roses, a tune takes flight,
Crimson blooms dance in moonlight.
They strum their petals like guitars,
Singing ballads to the stars.

But thorns are sharp and joke around,
"Watch your step, don't hit the ground!"
The laughter echoes through the night,
As roses twirl with pure delight!

Opus of the Orchard

In the orchard, apples chat,
Hats on squirrels, just like that.
Bees wear glasses, buzz with flair,
While singing birds dance in the air.

Pies are winking, rolling by,
With whipped cream clouds up in the sky.
The trees gossip, roots entwined,
As peaches tell tales of the past, unconfined.

Cherries juggle, lemons cheer,
Grapes debate what wine is near.
Every branch a lively show,
Where laughter blooms and breezes blow.

So come and join this merry spree,
In fruit-filled fun, so wild and free.
Each bite a giggle, sweet and bright,
In this orchard, all is light.

Elysium of Echoes

In the hills where echoes play,
Balloons debate which way to sway.
Jokes float high, like kites in flight,
As shadows chase the fading light.

A llama sings a funny tune,
While juggling daisies, oh what a boon!
Waves of laughter crash ashore,
As rainbows giggle, wanting more.

Mirrors tease with silly tricks,
Pranks unfold in sound's quick flicks.
The sun wears shades, quite dapper too,
While the moon grins with a winking view.

In this realm where humor thrives,
Every echo keeps joy alive.
So step right up and take a chance,
In the land where giggles dance.

Ambers of Autumn

Leaves swirl and dance, all around,
Squirrels chase nuts that hit the ground.
Pumpkins wear smiles, wide and bright,
While ghosts tell jokes in the pale moonlight.

Cider's a-fizz, just like my thoughts,
With every sip, my worries forgot.
Witches brew laughter, a bubbling delight,
As scarecrows chuckle, taking flight.

Euphony in Desolation

The wind sings out, a humorous tune,
While cacti wear crowns, under the moon.
Desert's dry laugh echoes in sand,
Where tumbleweeds dance, unplanned.

Rattlesnakes joke, they wiggle and sway,
With each tiny trill, the critters play.
Cacti get jealous of the sun's hot glow,
As shades of mirth grow, don't you know?

Rhapsody of Risings

Balloons float up, in colors so bright,
Chasing the sun, what a silly sight!
Laughter erupts, as kids take flight,
In a world where clouds are soft and light.

Kites zigzag high, in the playful breeze,
Making silly shapes, with perfect ease.
Every rise and dip is a giggling cheer,
As dreams take off, with no fear near.

Poems of Petal's Fall

Petals flutter down, like tiny songs,
As bees buzz by, just where it belongs.
Flowers shake hands before they sleep,
In a slumber party, secrets they keep.

A rose wears glasses, quite the sight,
With daisies that giggle with all their might.
As petals descend, they can't help but tease,
In the garden of laughs, there's no need to freeze.

Cantata of the Cactus Blossoms

In a desert, cacti smile,
With arms wide, they dance a while.
Their flowers bloom, a jest so bright,
Singing jokes in the moonlight.

Prickles tickle at every turn,
Who knew plants could be so stern?
With laughter shared under the sun,
Their dry wit is simply fun.

When rain arrives, they sing and sway,
Wet petals getting in the way.
A party for those tough and bold,
With stories of the desert told.

So here's to flowers, sharp and proud,
Providing giggles, loud and loud.
In sandy realms, they find their cheer,
A hilarious team, year after year.

Lyrical Hues of the Hibiscus

Hibiscus blooms in shades so grand,
They wander through the sunlit land.
With laughter bursting from each petal,
A floral joke, both light and metal.

Their colors clash in joyful glee,
A carnival of hue, you see.
Butterflies laugh as they glide past,
In a world where color's unsurpassed.

The breeze whispers secrets bright,
Hibiscus blooms in pure delight.
Tickling the leaves, they sway and spin,
Whimsical wonders, let the fun begin.

In gardens filled with vibrant hues,
Their antics brighten even the blues.
With every smile, they twist and twine,
Clever blossoms, the stars they shine.

Rhapsody of the Rustic Bloom

Rustic flowers play a tune,
Underneath the lazy moon.
With petals that dance in the breeze,
They mischief in the shady trees.

Dandelions, bold little jesters,
Giggle as the wind attests to.
They scatter seeds like silly dreams,
Painting fields with golden beams.

Forget-me-nots start to prance,
In every patch, they steal the chance.
They wink and nod, so sly and spry,
Holding onto fun, they can't deny.

Thus blooms the choir, wild and free,
In melody, the joy we see.
Rustic and cheerful, they rise to play,
A rhapsody of bright bouquet!

Chronicles of the Evening Primrose

Evening primrose, soft and sweet,
Telling tales of nightly meet.
With petals yawning, they stretch wide,
Whispers of laughter, side by side.

A moonlit drama, bright and bold,
As stories of the night unfold.
They chuckle when the stars appear,
Sharing secrets only they hear.

Blooming quick, then fading fast,
An epic of shadows they cast.
With every wink, a playful tease,
Evening tales that aim to please.

Their chronicles, a joyful sight,
In the softest shade of night.
With every flicker, every rhyme,
Primrose sings of fun through time.

Verses from the Violet Meadow

In a meadow of violet, a goat wore a hat,
He danced with a duck, who was friendly and fat.
They twirled and they spun, causing quite the scene,
As flowers giggled softly, with petals of green.

A squirrel in spectacles, reading a tome,
Declared to the crowd, 'This meadow's my home!'
With acorns for ink, he wrote tales of delight,
While butterflies fluttered, all day and all night.

Stanzas of the Sunflower's Smile

The sunflowers chuckled, their faces so bright,
Tickling the clouds with their petals of light.
A bumblebee buzzed, with a wig on askew,
He made quite a fuss, looking fancy and new.

A turtle in a tutu, spun round with flair,
The sunflowers cheered, sent laughter in the air.
'Oh, dance with us!' they urged, in their joyful cheer,
As the breeze whispered secrets for all to hear.

Odes to the Orchid's Opulence

In a garden of orchids, shiny and grand,
A parrot with pearls perched upon a hand.
He squawked out a sonnet, as purple vines twirled,
While a snail in a bow tie oozed past on his world.

With petals like velvet, they put on a show,
An ant in a tuxedo joined in with a bow.
'The poshest of flowers,' you might hear them say,
As the orchids just giggled, endearing their way.

Echoes from the Elderflower

Among elderflowers, a rabbit wore shades,
He told silly tales of his summertime wades.
With carrots as microphones, he'd strut and he'd preen,
While birds formed a band, their feathers pristine.

A hedgehog, quite dapper, joined in on the fun,
He juggled three berries, then slipped on a bun.
With laughter erupting, from bush to sweet tree,
The echoes rang clearly, wild and carefree.

Whispers of the Wildflowers

In the meadow, flowers chat,
A daisy wears a silly hat.
The poppies tease the bumblebees,
While daisies dance in the playful breeze.

Lilies laugh at passing ants,
While tulips twirl in fancy pants.
A sunflower grins with sunny glee,
As grasshoppers join in, oh what a spree!

The violets tell a joke so bright,
Petal pals giggle through the night.
They plan a dance, it'll be a blast,
In the wildflower field, their joy will last.

With every bloom and playful tease,
Nature's humor flows with ease.
So let your heart delight and sway,
In the wildflowers' fanciful play.

Serenade of the Starlit Sky

Underneath the moon's soft glow,
Stars make wishes, dancing slow.
A comet zooms in sparkly sight,
While twinkling stars giggle with delight.

The owls hoot a cheeky rhyme,
As fireflies join in the rhythm of time.
A meteor shower, what a scene,
Lighting up the night, all fresh and clean.

Overhead, the constellations grin,
Laughing at the silly things we spin.
Every wink and shimmer in the night,
Keeps the universe feeling light.

So raise a toast to this cosmic show,
In starlit laughter, let your spirit flow.
With jokes from the sun and wishes from the moon,
Join in the serenade; we'll dance until noon.

Melodies Beneath the Maple

Beneath the maple, laughter stirs,
With chirping birds and fluffy furs.
A squirrel jests about his stash,
While leaves do pirouettes in a flash.

The breeze hums tunes of days gone by,
As acorns tumble, oh my, oh my!
Chirping crickets join the play,
Singing melodies in a lively way.

The branches sway to nature's song,
As all the woodland friends come along.
A raccoon winks with a cheeky grin,
While the fireflies flash, and the fun begins.

So beneath this maple, take a seat,
Join the melody, feel the beat.
With every rustle and glimmer of light,
Laugh with the forest, it's pure delight!

Echoes of the Garden's Heart

In the garden, laughter grows,
With buzzing bees and fragrant shows.
The roses giggle, petals blush,
While marigolds join in with a hush.

Tomatoes wink from their leafy bed,
As cabbages boast and dance ahead.
The carrots chuckle beneath the ground,
While pepper plants sway all around.

With every sprinkle and morning dew,
The garden sings of joy untrue.
A rabbit hops, wearing a crown,
Making sure no frowns are found.

So stroll through this paradise unique,
Where flowers and veggies play hide and seek.
In the echoes of the garden's heart,
Find humor and love, a perfect art.

Echoes of the Evening

In the twilight's playful breeze,
A cat sings songs from the trees.
With each meow, the stars align,
Belting ballads, oh so fine.

A squirrel joins with tiny drums,
The chorus swells, here comes the fun!
Old owls hoot, a jazzy beat,
Nature's band, can't feel my feet!

Laughter drifts on starlit air,
Dancing shadows everywhere.
Fireflies twirl, a light ballet,
Evening joins the grand cabaret.

And in this silly serenade,
Every ballad glows, displayed.
Mirthful echoes fill the night,
As giggles spread, oh what a sight!

Petals of the Past

Once I planted seeds of whim,
Forgot to water, what a sin!
Petals burst, with laughter loud,
Brightly shaming me, I bowed.

Old stories shared from yesterday,
With blooms that dance and laugh and sway.
Each tale a petal, crisp and bright,
Spinning yarns 'til we take flight.

A dandelion's wish goes by,
Whispers of dreams, oh how they fly!
I chase them down, fall in the mud,
Covered in giggles, and flower buds.

Memories flutter, odd and true,
Like mismatched socks, like skies of blue.
In the garden where mirth and glee,
Plant the roots of history!

Serenade of Sunsets

As day bids night a silly kiss,
Colors swirl in a humorous bliss.
Orange and pink, they wink and tease,
While crickets tune up with ease.

Stretched out clouds play peek-a-boo,
With silly shapes to surprise you.
"Look! A dog!" I shout in delight,
"Oh wait! It's just a dandelion in flight."

The sun slides down like a clown in shade,
With rosy cheeks, it's a masquerade.
Don't let the twilight take its due,
Join the chorus, sing something new!

Wander into the evening glow,
Chasing shadows, storming the show.
Life's a stage with laughter's cue,
A serenade meant just for you!

Harmonies of Heartstrings

Pluck the strings of silly dreams,
As laughter bursts like sunny beams.
With every note, the giggles roll,
A melody that trolls the soul.

Ducks in bow ties quack offbeat,
While turtles dance on wobbling feet.
Harmony found in wacky play,
Strumming joy that leads the way.

Frogs croon blues by the lake side,
With croaks that swell like tides of pride.
Swaying flowers join in tune,
With petals twirling, oh what a swoon!

Let heartstrings twine in playful fray,
As jigs of life lead us astray.
In this dance with laughter's thread,
We find the joy that's daily fed!

Cantatas of the Clouds

In the sky, the clouds do dance,
They waltz and spin, not a chance.
One wears a hat, the other a shoe,
Singing tunes that sound like moo.

A fluffy fellow drifts on by,
Claims he's a bird, oh my, oh my!
A stormy party, what a sight,
Lightning strikes, then takes a flight.

Cotton candy or a big ice cream,
These puffy pals just love to dream.
Chasing rainbows, silly and free,
While thunder grumbles with a tee-hee.

Clouds giggle, sprinkle raindrops too,
A shower of laughs for me and you.
When the sun beams with a wink,
They scatter smiles—what do you think?

Reflections of the Raindrop

Raindrops dance on the window pane,
Rolling down like a playful train.
One drop shouts, 'I'm the fastest here!'
While others giggle, 'Go grab a beer!'

Splashes jump from puddles so round,
Making music, a joyful sound.
Each droplet sings in a juicy jive,
The rhythm of rain keeps us alive.

A raindrop slips and shimmies wide,
On a dog's nose, it takes a ride.
The pup sneezes, oh what a sight,
Raindrops laugh, 'That pup's a fright!'

When the sun comes out with a grin,
The drops play hide and seek again.
They wave goodbye, with a tilt and toss,
'Next time we'll party—who's the boss?'

Sagas of the Saffron

In the spice garden, saffron blooms,
It tickles noses, fills the rooms.
A pinch of laughter in each dish,
Makes your curry dance and swish.

A saffron sprout swears it's a star,
'Look at my hue, I've come so far!'
The garlic snickers, 'Oh please, my friend,
You're just a spice, this is the end!'

In the kitchen, pots bubble with glee,
A chef waltzes, 'Come taste, you'll see!'
Chili peppers scream, 'Not too hot!'
While the saffron flirts, 'I'm the top slot!'

With every meal, they tell a tale,
Funny flavors that never fail.
The saffron grins, 'I'll spice your way!'
And all the veggies start to play.

Weavings of Wonder

In a land where the yarns do talk,
Threads of joy on a merry walk.
A blue string says, 'I'm the sky!'
While the green replies, 'Oh my, oh my!'

A tapestry spins tales of cheer,
Of bunnies and bears that drink root beer.
Every stitch holds a giggle or grin,
As the fabric whispers, 'Let's begin!'

Silken dreams in colors so bright,
Knitting wishes both day and night.
A purl of laughter, a cast-off sigh,
As the needles wink, 'We will fly high!'

With whimsy and flair, they weave away,
Creating wonders, come what may.
In this world of threads and twine,
Every fiber's dance is simply divine!

Soliloquies of the Stars

In a sky of twinkling lights,
The stars gossip, day and night.
One says, 'I'm a shooting star!'
The others chuckle, 'You ain't that far!'

They dance around in cosmic glee,
Telling tales of a moonlit spree.
'Have you seen that bright-eyed comet?'
'Not yet, but I'll bet he'll flaunt it!'

When meteors fall with trails of fire,
They all shout, 'Time to retire!'
With wishes tossed and dreams galore,
The sky laughs until they're sore!

And when the dawn arrives to play,
They disappear, a bright ballet.
But one cheeky star, with a wink,
Says, 'See you all, I've got to blink!'

Rhyme among the Roses

In a garden where petals sway,
Roses gather for a play.
One yells, 'I've got a pun to share!'
Another whispers, 'I don't care!'

They tell jokes about thorns and stems,
Laughing loudly, making gems.
'Why did the flower join a band?'
'To make some lovely music, understand?'

Then a bee buzzes, 'What's the buzz?'
Roses giggle, 'It's all just fuzz!'
With every wink and every sway,
They embrace the bright sunny ray.

As the sun dips low and shadows creep,
Roses snicker, then fall asleep.
Dreams of laughter fill the air,
In this garden, joy is everywhere!

Harmonies in the Haze

In the mist where whispers roam,
Voices blend to find a home.
One sings, 'Can you hear that tune?'
The rest reply, 'It's off the moon!'

With echoes of laughter in the air,
They make jokes without a care.
'Why did the fog go to school?'
'To learn the tricks, and be a fool!'

A melody floats through the foggy night,
They dance around, feeling light.
'What's that over there—a shadow fine?'
'Just a breeze, stealing our time!'

As dawn breaks and the haze recedes,
They promise to meet, planting seeds.
In laughter and song, they'll appear,
To play in harmony, year after year!

Parchments of the Past

Old pages whisper tales of yore,
Of knights and jesters, legends galore.
One parchment sighs, 'I need a drink!'
Another laughs, 'Just read and think!'

They speak of kings who danced in masks,
And queens with far too many tasks.
'Why did the scribe write all night?'
'So he could win an ink-filled fight!'

As dust swirls like a playful breeze,
They giggle among the ancient trees.
'These stories make no sense at all!'
'Ah, but they surely make us laugh and sprawl!'

When morning comes, they'll still remain,
Entwined in laughter, shadow, and rain.
For every tale that's ever passed,
Finds joy in the echoes of the past!

Chiming Chimes of Grace

In a garden where laughter grows,
The chimes jingle with silly prose.
A squirrel dances with a light step,
While the flowers giggle, no one inept.

A frog croaks jokes by the old pond,
With a crown made of leafy frond.
The breeze carries creamy whip,
As the bees join in on the quip.

The sun rolls like a golden coin,
Tickling the petals, cheerful and joint.
Rabbits hop with hats and flair,
Combining mischief with fresh spring air.

At dusk, the stars twinkle in pride,
While fireflies dance and coincide.
Each note rings out, a merry tease,
In this garden, everyone's at ease.

Driftwood Dialogues

On a shore where driftwood chats,
Seagulls squabble, the kings of brats.
One stick claims to have washed ashore,
While a barnacle tells tales galore.

The shells gossip in soft, hushed tones,
While waves laugh, tossing out their moans.
A jellyfish hums an off-key tune,
As crabs jiggle beneath the moon.

Sandcastles await the tides' big show,
With towers of laughter, all aglow.
The ocean tickles with every wave,
Inviting all us, the merry and brave.

And when the sun sets, shadows sway,
The driftwood sighs, it's time to play.
With stories sprouting, breezy and bright,
Driftwood dialogues last all night.

Starlit Serenades

Under the sky where giggles grow,
The stars twinkle, putting on a show.
A comet zips with a wink and a wave,
While planets chuckle, cosmic and brave.

The moon beamed down on a vagrant tune,
As night critters danced in a merry swoon.
Fireflies flicker in a winking spree,
Lighting the way for the giggling spree.

Owls hoot their best stand-up lines,
While crickets chirp in perfect rhymes.
Each breeze comes in with a funny jest,
In starlit serenades, we are blessed.

With the universe spinning and swirling around,
Nature's humor is perfectly bound.
Under twinkling stars, we grin and sway,
Embracing each laugh at the end of the day.

Ballads in the Breeze

In a meadow alive with chirpy delight,
The flowers sway with all of their might.
A butterfly flutters by, in a swirl,
Whispering secrets with a twirling twirl.

The trees lean in, with rustling leaves,
Sharing tall tales that nobody believes.
A breeze runs through, like a cheeky friend,
Playing pranks until you must bend.

Dandelions puff with laughter so loud,
As the clouds shape-shift into a crowd.
With hiccuping giggles from skies up high,
Kites dance and tumble, almost fly.

So come join the fun, let joy unleash,
With ballads carried in the softest breeze.
Let nature's whimsy break every norm,
In this whimsical world, we'll always swarm.

Lullabies of the Lavender Breeze

A cat wore a hat, such a sight,
He danced in the garden, pure delight.
The flowers giggled under the sun,
As bees joined the party, oh what fun!

A dog on a skateboard, wheeled around,
Chasing butterflies that flit and bound.
With every turn, he gave a bark,
While squirrels played tag in the park.

A turtle in shoes tried to race,
He tripped on his laces, what a disgrace!
The rabbits all laughed, rolled on the grass,
As the frog played the fiddle, a charming brass.

So let's sing a tune, silly and bright,
With laughter and joy, we'll dance through the night.
For in this garden, we'll find a way,
To sprinkle our lives with humor each day!

Sonnet of the Silver Springs

A fish in the pond wore a crown so wide,
He thought he was royal, a noble guide.
He swam with a wink, so full of cheer,
While frogs croaked their songs, sincere and clear.

The ducks all quacked jokes, with flair and finesse,
While turtles rolled dice in a game of excess.
A picnic was planned on the soft, green banks,
Where everyone laughed, shared their funny pranks.

A squirrel tossed acorns like bombs from above,
While a raccoon danced slyly, all covered in love.
With tales of mischief, they lightened the air,
In this whimsical place, joy's everywhere!

So join in the fun, laughter's the key,
In the silver springs, where we're wild and free.
The humor abounds, let your worries cease,
For this merry gathering brings only peace!

Rhythms of the Rain-soaked Petals

A snail with a sax played a jazzy tune,
While raindrops drummed softly, a sweet afternoon.
The flowers swayed gently to the beat's embrace,
As puddles reflected a giggling face.

A frog leapt about in a slick, shiny coat,
He slipped with a splash while trying to float.
The daisies all snickered as raindrops fell down,
Hats made of petals adorned his small crown.

A ladybug waltzed with a soft little beetle,
Their moves sent the crowd into laughter's cathedral.
With rhythms and jokes, they shared all their charms,
In the rain-soaked petals, dance held us in arms.

So gather your friends, come join this parade,
Where silliness blooms and sun showers invade.
Through the laughter and joy, let this moment play,
In the heart of the garden, let fun lead the way!

Harmonies in Hummingbird Flight

A hummingbird strummed on a string of bright light,
Causing flowers to giggle, oh what a sight!
With wings like confetti, he danced in the air,
Sipping sweet nectar, without a care.

A beetle played bongo, tapping his feet,
While ants marched along in a rhythmic beat.
The petals all clapped, joining in the fun,
As they twirled in the breeze, beneath the warm sun.

A butterfly juggled, with grace and with flair,
Three tiny seeds, flying here and there.
The crowd laughed along, as blooms cheered him on,
In this merry moment, where worries are gone.

So let's lift our voices, let laughter ignite,
For in this small garden, everything feels right.
With harmony found in the fluttering flight,
We'll dance through the day, embracing the light!

Chronicles of the Canopy

Up in the trees, a squirrel sent a tweet,
With nuts on his mind, he couldn't be beat.
He danced on a branch with a caffeinated flair,
And laughed at the owls who were caught unaware.

A parrot chimed in, with a voice oh so bright,
"Who needs a good meal when you've got this delight?"
He wore a top hat and a monocle too,
As he juggled some berries for the forest crew.

The raccoon just grinned, with mischief his friend,
He pocketed snacks, claiming, "I'll share in the end!"
The laughter erupted as they all took a stand,
In the game of the day, they were close-knit and grand.

Tonic of Twilights

At dusk in the park, the fireflies waltz,
With sparkles that bounce like unexpected faults.
A frog sings a tune in a tuxedo of green,
While mice in small suits join the evening scene.

The moon blinks a wink from its throne in the sky,
As crickets compose an amusing lullaby.
The wind plays the flute, and leaves join the beat,
They dance with abandon on this twilight street.

A raccoon in disguise, with a cap and a cane,
Claims he's the mayor of this wild, funny lane.
He adjusts his fake glasses, so proud and so spry,
While the frogs burst in laughter and leap ever high.

Fragments of Flora

In a garden so bright, flowers whisper and giggle,
Petunias tell tales that make daisies wiggle.
A sunflower grinned, reaching high for a laugh,
While roses rolled over, too pleased to do math.

Tulips wear tutus, a sight quite absurd,
They pirouette freely, joy is their word.
"Let's throw a grand party!" the violets declare,
Soon friends of all colors fill up the air.

A dandelion floats, teasing winds with a grin,
"Who knew being wild would bring so much win?"
The petals all cheered as they swayed and they spun,
In a floral fiesta, where laughter's the fun.

Rhythms of Raindrops

Pitter-patter echoes, a tap dance on roofs,
Each drop tells a story, and nature approves.
A puddle reflects all the clouds in a race,
While kids in bright boots prepare for the chase.

Raindrops in rhythm create a sweet song,
As they tumble and bubble, all night long.
A giggling kid splashes, "Oh, take that you rain!"
Turning grey skies to laughter, deleting all pain.

A snail slicked in silver, sliding by with a grin,
"Join the festivity, let the fun begin!"
Umbrellas like mushrooms sprout in delight,
As nature's own party comes alive in the night.

Harmonies on the Hilltop

On the hilltop, cows do sing,
They moo in tune, a funny thing.
The sheep join in with leaps and bounds,
A chorus found in grassy grounds.

A goat with flair, a caper queen,
Dances round in a silly scene.
Beneath the sun, they prance and play,
Together brightening the day.

A chicken clucks a merry rhyme,
While rabbits hop in perfect time.
Each creature knows their part, oh dear,
Their harmonies bring laughter near.

At sunset's glow, they end the show,
With rhymes of life, they surely know.
The hilltop ring with giggles soar,
A symphony forevermore.

Verses at Dawn's Edge

At dawn's edge, the roosters crow,
With sleepy eyes, they steal the show.
A pig trots by, in stripes of pink,
Belly flopping, quick as a wink.

The sun peeks up, a golden eye,
As ducks parade in line, oh my!
A quack or two bursts in the air,
Feathers flying everywhere.

Bumbling bees begin to hum,
A buzzing band, a morning drum.
A cat with shades takes on the stage,
His sassy strut brings all the rage.

Each dawn unfolds new antics bright,
In verses where the world's all right.
With laughter rich and joy in flight,
The day begins, oh, what a sight!

Phrases of the Prairie

In the prairie, grasses sway,
As bunnies frolic, come what may.
A tumbleweed rolls on the ground,
With giggles echoing all around.

A cowboy hat, too large, it seems,
Falls on a llama, crushing dreams.
With every kick and funny stare,
They spin about without a care.

The cacti dance, arms in the air,
While javelinas pretend to care.
With snorts and snickers, they keep the beat,
As nature joins in on this comedic feat.

The golden sun laughs on each face,
In this prairie, all find their place.
With phrases spun in laughter's thread,
In every heart, a smile is fed.

Echoes of the Evergreen

In evergreens, the whispers play,
With branches swaying, come what may.
A squirrel tells a joke so fine,
While all the birds in chorus whine.

A bear in glasses reads a book,
Next to a fox with quite the look.
They share a laugh, a funny tale,
As nature's joy begins to scale.

Pinecone bombs dropped from up high,
Make the rabbits jump and sigh.
With goofy hops and playful spins,
The echoes laugh as fun begins.

As twilight falls, the stars shine bright,
In evergreens, through the night.
These echoes weave through every leaf,
A melody of purest brief.

Tales Among the Tulips

In a garden where flowers giggle and sway,
Tulips tell tales in a colorful play.
With whispers of wind, they sway to and fro,
A dance on the petals, a vibrant show.

Bees buzz with laughter, a comedic hum,
They trade funny stories with a sprightly drum.
Daisies join in with their dainty delight,
Chasing the butterflies, they take to flight.

An ant in a top hat, quite dapper and bold,
Tells jokes to the daisies, their giggles unfold.
While ladybugs chuckle and tickle the grass,
Even the roses can't help but laugh en masse.

So come to the garden, where fun's never shy,
These flowered comedians will brighten your sky.
With laughter like petals, the joy it instills,
In the heart of the blooms, humor's sweet thrills.

Melodic Motifs of the Moon

Under a moon that winks with a grin,
Crickets croon tunes that flutter and spin.
A frog on a lily pad claims he's a star,
Ribbiting ballads that travel afar.

Owls hoot in harmony, a comical choir,
While clouds play a game, becoming a tire.
The stars twinkle softly, chuckling with glee,
At the antics of night, oh what sights to see!

The wind tells a story of silly mischief,
As fireflies giggle, their laughter's a gift.
Moonlight's a jester, with beams of pure fun,
Painting the night till the morning has come.

So dance 'neath the shimmer, let laughter abound,
In melodies merry, let joy be unbound.
Each note in the night, a spark of delight,
With the moon as our muse, we're friends with the night.

Reveries of the Rhubarb

In the patch of the rhubarb, mischief does grow,
With leaves full of stories, and laughter in tow.
A sprout tells of veg that once tried to sing,
But an onion's due cries made their voices take wing.

Carrots wear sunglasses, all cool and aloof,
While radishes roll and make quite a goof.
An elder chard chuckles, he's wise and he's bright,
He's seen all the laughs that sprout from the night.

The turnips are chuckling, their roots intertwined,
They dance in their beds, having fun, unconfined.
With rhubarb as ringleader, it's quite the affair,
They throw a grand party, with joy in the air.

So join in the revel, where veggies unite,
With jokes and with rhythms, the laughs are a sight.
In the heart of the garden, with smiles on display,
The rhubarb will cheer you to dance and to play.

Chants of the Cherries

In the orchard of cherries, the laughter is sweet,
With each bouncing berry, they skip on their feet.
Red fruits with chortles, in the sunshine they glow,
Their giggles like raindrops, in breezy flow.

A wise cherry elder, with wrinkles and flair,
Tells tales of the squirrels, who dance in midair.
While branches all shimmy, and leaves rustle loud,
The cherries are joyful, a jolly red crowd.

A game of hide and seek, they giggle and squeal,
As the sun dips low, it's a playful appeal.
With shadows that stretch, creating a scene,
Each cherry's a star in a comedy green.

So frolic with cherries, let laughter ignite,
In their merry embrace, feel the joy, pure and bright.
With feelings so fruity, a whimsical cheer,
In the garden of giggles, come join us, my dear.

Tapestry of Tides

A crab wore a hat, oh what a sight,
He danced on the beach, by day and by night.
Seagulls all chuckled, they joined in the play,
Who knew crabs had grooves, they danced all day!

The waves brought in jelly, a jiggling friend,
He bounced on the shore, again and again.
With each little splash, he caused quite a scene,
The funniest fish you've ever seen!

A starfish told jokes, with arms wide and free,
He tickled the octopus, full of glee.
They rolled in the sand, all covered in foam,
Turning the beach into a wild home!

So when the tide shifts, and the sun starts to fade,
Remember the laughter, the memories made.
For the sea is a stage, where the funny reside,
In this wild waltz, let joy be your guide.

Echoed Emotions

In a town filled with echoes, each wall had a tale,
A parrot named Polly would squawk without fail.
She'd mimic the gossip, the laughter, the gripes,
Turning the dull into whimsical types!

A dog in a bow tie would dance on the street,
With paws like a pro, he could't be beat.
The pigeons all watched, with heads cocked to side,
As laughter erupted, they took it in stride.

One night at the park, under moon's silver glow,
A cat played the fiddle, stealing the show.
The mice formed a band, with pie tins and spoons,
Creating a symphony that swayed to the tunes.

So listen, dear friend, to the laughter around,
Where echoes of joy are eagerly found.
In a world full of whimsy, where smiles never tire,
Let every emotion be a note on a lyre.

Symphonies of Silence

In a library quiet, where dust bunnies glide,
A mouse with a book opened wide, could not hide.
He whispered a giggle, so soft and so sweet,
While the cat snoozed beside him, with dreams at his feet.

A turtle in glasses, so wise and so slow,
Pondered the meaning of cheese – do you know?
With each thoughtful pause, all the critters fell still,
Waiting for answers, for wisdom to spill.

In the corner, a parakeet made a funny face,
He danced to the stillness, with great, silly grace.
While the shadows chuckled at the jokes in their midst,
This symphony of silence couldn't be missed.

So wander the quiet, where laughter is shy,
And let every chuckle be a secret reply.
For in softest whispers, where giggles reside,
Is a harmony hidden, full of whimsical pride.

Whispers of the Woods

In the forest so green, the owls spun a yarn,
Of a fox in a tutu, who danced on the lawn.
With twirls and with hops, he stole every glance,
Leaving critters in stitches, all lost in his dance.

The squirrels went nuts, they couldn't stop laughing,
As the rabbit stood still, secretly crafting.
A crown made of leaves, so wobbly and fine,
Turned him into king, for one fleeting time!

But a raccoon in shades had a plot up his sleeve,
He planned a great heist, but oh what a weave!
When he reached for the prize, a pie meant for a feast,
He slipped on a acorn, and roared like a beast!

So gather your friends, let the woods hear your cheer,
For in nature's embrace, there's laughter near here.
In whispers and rustles, let joy be your hood,
In the heart of the forest, come dance if you could!

Lyricism of Larks

Larks in the park, they sing so loud,
Chasing the sun, they dance in a crowd.
With each little chirp, they crack silly jokes,
While dodging the cats that stalk like sly folks.

In the great green field, they've made a nest,
Planning their pranks, they surely are blessed.
One lark wears a hat that's way too big,
While another's still learning to do a jig.

They try to impress with their offbeat tones,
But clash with the frogs and their croaky moans.
Conspiracy brews over worms on the ground,
As larks plot delight, laughter's spread all around.

So raise your glass high to these jesters in flight,
With antics so silly, they brighten the night.
Whistle along, join their humorous spree,
In a world full of larks, there's no misery.

Narratives of the Nightshade

In the twilight gloom, the nightshade pranks,
With whispers of secrets and mischievous winks.
They plot and they plan in their shadowy lair,
Causing giggles and chuckles, beyond compare.

Once a raccoon wore a mask from the vines,
Thinking he'd blend in with shimmers and shines.
But nightshade's laughter was hard to conceal,
As the raccoon tripped on a slippery wheel.

A tale unfolds, where shadows collide,
As nightshade plants sings in the dark where they hide.
Their tales of absurdity make spirits uplift,
With every twist and turn, life becomes a gift.

So raise a toast to the stories they weave,
In moonlit mischief, where all hearts believe.
With nightshade's delight, let the laughter ring,
For every sly prank brings a joy that they bring.

Cadence of Cerulean Skies

Under cerulean skies, the clouds play a game,
Fluffing and pouting, they all share a name.
One clouds just floats by, with an oversized grin,
While others do somersaults, ready to spin.

A thunderbolt grumbles, tries cracking a joke,
But the wind turns around, and up goes the smoke.
Raindrops chuckle, take turns on the slide,
While light rays join in, beaming bright with pride.

In the comedy show of the vast sapphire expanse,
Each gust holds a secret, each breeze takes a chance.
A kite flutters by, with a wink and a swerve,
How it dances through azure, oh, what a verve!

So laugh loud and high, with the skies as your stage,
In the cadence of colors, let joy be your gauge.
For under cerulean, there's laughter galore,
Just look to the heavens and let your heart soar.

Ballads of the Brave Blossoms

Brave blossoms stand tall, in gardens they thrive,
Each petal's a story, keeping dreams alive.
They gossip of sunshine and chirp of the rain,
With snickers and giggles, they shun all the pain.

One daisy wore shades, thought it quite the scene,
While tulips just giggled, quite green with envy.
A bold little rose stood proud on her stem,
With thorns like a spire, she'd rule, yes, again!

In the sunlight's embrace, they boast and they cheer,
While bumblebees buzz, they bring up the rear.
Flirting with breezes, they sway 'neath the sky,
In the ballads of blooms, there's simply no why.

So dance with the petals, don't let life grow stale,
For brave blossoms know how to tell a grand tale.
In a garden of laughter, let hilarity bloom,
With each vibrant blossom, make room for more room!

Serenades in the Scented Shadow

In the garden, a gnome takes a nap,
Dreaming of tunes in a flowered cap.
The daisies dance, shaking their heads,
While the tulips giggle, all snug in their beds.

A bee with a trumpet is playing a tune,
Ignoring the rules of the afternoon.
With laughter around, all colors collide,
As petals declare there's no need to hide.

The wind hums a joke that makes all flowers blush,
Humorous whispers in every soft hush.
Roses, they chuckle, their thorns stand in plight,
While laughing sunflowers reach for the light.

In this fragrant realm, hilarity thrives,
Where even the butterflies dance in their jives.
A symphony of humor, so bright and so gay,
In the shadow of scents where the blossoms will play.

Paeans to the Peony's Grace

Oh, peony fair, with a pinkish grin,
You sit in the garden, where chaos begins.
Your petals are puffy, like clouds with a crown,
While ants wear tuxedos, they never frown.

The rabbits hop in, on a comedic spree,
Dressed up like jesters, what sights there will be!
With laughter like pollen that floats in the air,
The blooms conspire, in giggles they share.

Frogs croak in rhythm, with leaves as their stage,
The squirrels act out their acrobatic page.
While peonies blush from their leafy embrace,
As the garden erupts in a whimsical race.

With laughter and sunshine, the colors unite,
As petals applaud, what a curious sight!
The peony beams in this humor so vast,
With friendships in bloom, we'll have quite the blast.

The Anthem of the Azalea

Oh azalea bright, with your ruffled attire,
You summon the giggles, a lovely choir.
With hues that could tickle the hearts of the meek,
While rabbits toss jokes, in their playful peak.

The breeze carries laughter, a tickling sound,
As butterflies flirt, spinning 'round and 'round.
The daisies roll over, like kids on a swing,
In this riot of colors, each bloom starts to sing.

With every soft rustle, the garden's alive,
In whimsical rhythm, the flowers all thrive.
The sun gives a wink as the petals confess,
That humor in blooms is a sweet kind of mess.

And azaleas sway in their frolicsome dance,
Here, joy holds the reins, come and take a chance.
In a patch of pure laughter, let your heart roam,
For each flower knows this is truly our home.

Melodic Murmurs from the Moonflower

In the moonlit patch where the moonflower blooms,
The night holds a magic, casting out glooms.
With whispers like honey, the petals unwind,
Pulling in starlight, the laughter's aligned.

The crickets compose with their chirpy delight,
While owls crack jokes in the soft, silver light.
But watch for the raccoons, they plan their heist,
Stealing the shine, not thinking twice!

With giggling fireflies dancing in glee,
The moonflower smiles, saying, "Look at me!"
With curls and with twirls, as the shadows parade,
They'll flaunt their bright petals in a grand masquerade.

In the garden's embrace, with the stars up above,
There's humor in silence, and laughter to love.
So linger a moment; the night seems to know,
That joy blooms eternal in this funny show.

Interludes in the Orchard

Under the tree, where apples blend,
A squirrel danced, quite round the bend.
He tripped on roots, a sight to see,
Declared himself, the king of spree.

Gathered friends, with nuts in hand,
They formed a troupe, a woodland band.
With acorn hats and leafy ties,
They sang of pies and sunny skies.

The farmer stopped, with chuckles loud,
As squirrels pranced, lured by the crowd.
"Who knew," he mused, with grin so wide,
"Those critters had such joyful pride!"

And so they danced till twilight's fall,
In that orchard where laughter called.
Each nutty note, a serenade,
In their kingdom, none could invade.

Sonnet of the Seasons

Winter wore socks, both orange and blue,
Sledges were flying, and snowmen too.
But spring snuck in with a cheeky tease,
She made the flowers pop, much like a breeze.

Summer burped loudly, "Hey, pass the ice!"
While autumn chuckled, "Oh, isn't this nice?"
Leaves did the cha-cha, twirling with flair,
As squirrels scolded, "We want to share!"

Each season pranced, in playful delight,
Chasing the shadows, morning to night.
A dance-off commenced, with giggles so grand,
In a cycle of fun, hand in hand.

So raise your glass, to this merry crew,
Who take on the year, with laughter, it's true.
From snowy to sunny, they spin around,
In the merry-go-round where joy is found.

Ode to the Wildflowers

In a meadow bright, wild blooms abide,
They giggle and chatter, with breezes as guide.
Each petal a story, with colors so bold,
In the dance of the sun, their secrets unfold.

Dandelions blow, like whispers in flight,
Daring the clouds with laughter, alight.
"Oh dear," says the daisy, "what mischief we'll sow?"
"I'll tickle the bee, and watch him just go!"

Buttercups shimmer, like jewels in the grass,
While wise old clover, with glasses of glass,
Pondered the gossip of wind through the trees,
As petals all twirled, with leisurely ease.

The wildflowers grinned, as the day slipped away,
With a wink to the stars, they'd dance 'til the gray.
In patches of color, they spun tales anew,
In this festival of laughter, bright and true.

Refrains of the River

Down by the river, a turtle conspired,
To race with the fish, who all seemed inspired.
"Ready, set, splash!" with a flick of a fin,
As they paddled along, with big toothy grins.

But the otters, of course, were the ones in the lead,
With flips and with flops, they proceeded with speed.
"Oh dear," sighed the turtle, "I'll need a new plan,
Perhaps I'll just float, till I catch up, if I can!"

The reeds chuckled softly, the stones rolled their eyes,
As the river kept flowing with giggles and sighs.
Fish tales grew taller, like reeds in the breeze,
"Last week, I jumped over the great willow trees!"

In the joyful current, each creature would share,
In the rhythm of life, and the tales in the air.
A chorus of chuckles, from shore to the tide,
Where laughter and water would ever abide.

A Tapestry of Tulip Tales

In the garden, blooms can dance,
Tulips giggle, given the chance.
With a sprinkle of sunny cheer,
They gossip loud for all to hear.

Beneath the sky, a playful show,
Petals prance, and breezes blow.
Each color tells a silly jest,
These flowers jest, they know the best.

A red one winks at yellow bright,
"Who's the fairest, day or night?"
While purple rolls in laughter wide,
"I'm the star, come take a ride!"

So next you stroll through blooms so wild,
Join in the jest! Be flower-child.
With tulip tales that never end,
Where every bloom is a zany friend.

Whimsy in the Wisteria's Whirl

Wisteria twirls in the breeze,
Spinning dreams like ribbons with ease.
"Catch me if you can!" they cheer,
As vines twist, laugh, and disappear.

Petals dangle, a playful swing,
Curly cues invite to fling.
A bumblebee joins in the game,
Buzzing tunes that sound the same.

One wisteria whispered quite low,
"Let's plant a riddle for the show!"
Each vine tangled in puzzlement,
Leaves all giggling at their intent.

So sway along with that soft vine,
In the whirl, your spirits'll shine.
With whimsy high and laughter pure,
The wisteria's joy feels so sure.

The Chorus of the Chrysanthemum

Chrysanthemums gather, a chatty crew,
They boast of shades both bright and blue.
In a laugh-off, they strive to peak,
Each bloom with tales that make you squeak.

"Oh, flower sock puppet!" one cries with glee,
"Your petals droop! You can't fool me!"
They giggle, twirl, a petal parade,
Winter's frost won't make them fade.

In the corner, a shy one lied,
"I've got a secret no one can hide."
But with a pop and little spout,
The truth came forth, and all found out.

So join the chorus, sing along,
With blooms so silly, it's hard to go wrong.
In jest they bloom, year after year,
Laughing in petals, spreading the cheer.

Nocturnal Notes of the Nightshade

Under moonlight, shadows dance bright,
Nightshade hums with pure delight.
"We're the kings and queens of the night,
Where all things funny take flight!"

Owls roll their eyes at flowered pranks,
Their giggles echo through the banks.
"Can you hear that silly tune?"
The nightshade giggles with the moon.

Bats swoop low with a flap and glide,
Joining in on the wacky ride.
"Who's the funniest in the glade?"
The nightshade shouts, "We're all made!"

So sway in the night with blooms so bold,
Together in laughter, stories unfold.
With nocturnal notes that never wane,
In nightshade's glow, joy does reign.

Lullabies in the Meadow

In a field of dreams, cows hum their tunes,
While bunnies throw parties beneath the bright moons.
Chickens in choir, they cluck and they flap,
As frogs in tuxedos decide to take naps.

Worms wear top hats, and crickets play sax,
Dancing in circles, they don't cut no tracks.
The sun starts to yawn, saying, 'Please don't be late!'
While daisies in gowns say, 'Let's celebrate!'

A pig with a banjo strums silly old songs,
The breeze joins the fun as it whistles along.
Butterflies twirl wearing glittery masks,
They giggle and flutter, forgetting their tasks.

The moon peeks in, wearing pajamas too,
And the stars join the chorus, they're singing to you.
With laughter and love, the night's not all bleak,
In this meadow of joy, every critter's unique.

Verses from the Vines

Through rows of the grapes, the bees make a buzz,
While squirrels throw parties, just because.
The grapes start to dance, wiggling with glee,
As the sunflower sways, 'Come dance with me!'

The rat in a sweater declares it's high time,
To spin silly tales in a jumbled up rhyme.
With chicken-shaped balloons and cupcakes to share,
The vines hold their breath in a sweet, breezy air.

A goat in a tux plays the fiddles so sweet,
While ladybugs laugh, tapping tiny bee feet.
The vines whisper secrets as shadows grow long,
Turning the vineyard into a song.

Rabbits in waistcoats hop down the lane,
While the grapevines chime in with a soft refrain.
A festival here where the laughter is free,
And every vine shares its fun melody.

Dance of the Daisies

In a meadow where daisies do wobble and sway,
They twirl with delight, in their bright blooms they play.
A sunflower leads with a grand, leafy flourish,
While ants bring the rhythm, their march never skirmish.

The butterflies giggle, they spin in the air,
While ladybugs wave, dancing without a care.
A rabbit with rhythm hops louder each beat,
As the daisies below cheer his two thumping feet.

The breeze joins the fun, tickling petals so bright,
As colors blend beautifully, pure sheer delight.
Caterpillars clap, making beats with their heads,
While the daisies grow dizzy, in whimsical threads.

At the end of the day, as the sun starts to sink,
The daisies all giggle, whispering, "Time to rethink!"
Each petal a tale, in their roots, they confide,
In the dance of the daisies, pure joy shall abide.

Melodies Among the Thorns

In a garden of thorns, where roses are grand,
A hedgehog recites poetry, clever and planned.
With giggles of roses all blushing with pride,
While the thorns give a chuckle, their prickles aside.

A snail with a trumpet, sounds jazzy and bold,
While daisies take notes, their petals unfold.
The laughter rolls on, like a wave in the night,
As critters convene for a harmonious flight.

Bees buzz around, in their polka-dot suits,
Carrying tunes in their sweet, honeyed roots.
The thorns start a jig, despite their own prick,
As the daisies jump in, with a whimsical flick.

In this thorny haven, where laughter's the king,
Even prickly companions can dance and can sing.
With every note sung, and every joke spun,
In the garden of melody, we all have our fun.

Whirlwinds of Wonder

In a world where socks can fly,
A chicken learned to make a pie.
The moon wears shades, what a sight!
Stars are dancing, feeling light.

Rainclouds giggle, make a mess,
Umbrellas turn to party dress.
A cat in boots comes strutting round,
Juggling fish, what a sound!

Bouncing bubbles, bouncing cheer,
Penguins tap dance, give a cheer.
A frog with shades, just lost his hat,
Chasing crickets, oh, imagine that!

Mice on scooters zoom away,
While frogs all join to sing and sway.
Laughs and giggles fill the air,
In this fun-filled, wacky affair!

Dances in the Dew

In the dawn, where dew drops play,
A snail competes in a ballet.
Worms are twirling, fancy feet,
All the critters can't be beat!

Fluffy rabbits join the song,
Hopping here, they can't go wrong.
The daisies sway, they clap along,
To the rhythm of the dawn's sweet song.

Ladybugs wear polka dots,
Flirting with the friendly spots.
Grasshoppers leap, a joyful sight,
Chasing sunbeams, pure delight!

As the sun begins to rise,
Fireflies blink, my oh my!
Nature's dancers, full of grace,
In this dew-filled, joyful place!

Voices of Violets

Violets chatter in the breeze,
Telling tales of insects' spree.
A wink from daisies, so divine,
Buzzing bees share laughter fine.

Butterflies wear costumes bright,
Swaying gently, pure delight.
A daffodil tries to sing,
While a grasshopper does his thing.

The petals gossip with the breeze,
Mimicking the swaying trees.
Their whispers echo through the glade,
As shadows dance in sun's parade.

At dusk, the colors softly blend,
The violets shout, it's time to mend.
In this garden, life's a spree,
Where voices mingle joyfully!

Murmurs in the Meadow

In the meadow, where all frolic free,
A cow sings opera with glee.
Sheep form a band, play their tunes,
While crickets dance beneath the moons.

A squirrel juggles acorns bright,
As rabbits hop, quite a sight.
The flowers rustle, share their perks,
While butterflies do silly quirks.

Grass blades tickle each passerby,
As peacocks strut, oh my oh my!
With laughter echoing far and wide,
In this meadow, joy's our guide.

When twilight falls, the fun won't cease,
The stars join in, they never freeze.
Murmurs of joy fill the air,
In this meadow, without a care!

Strokes of Serenity

In a garden where laughter grows,
The daisies dance in funny rows.
A squirrel tells jokes atop a tree,
While bumblebees play hide and seek with glee.

With every tickle of the breeze,
The blossoms giggle, if you please.
The grass blades hum a merry tune,
As butterflies twirl under the moon.

A snail slips on a slippery slide,
While others cheer, eyes open wide.
The sun winks as it starts to set,
In this serene, yet silly duet.

Cantos in the Clearing

Amidst the trees, a rumor spreads,
That frogs wear pants and ducks have dreads.
A caper in the clearing bright,
Where laughter echoes into the night.

A rabbit hops with style and flair,
Twirling in circles, without a care.
The chipmunks clap, they're quite a sight,
With tiny hats, all snug and tight.

They sing of cakes and pies galore,
While jesters juggle acorns and more.
The owl joins in with a wise crack,
And the moon beams down, alight, no lack.

Ballads Beneath the Boughs

Underneath the leafy dome,
A raucous rat claims it's his home.
He strums a tune with cheese-shaped picks,
Delivering laughs with clever tricks.

A band of mice in top hats parade,
While crickets chirp a serenade.
A dog digs deep to take a nap,
Yet wakes to dance, caught in the trap!

The shadows play a jolly game,
As fireflies join to light the fame.
With every note sung, joy rings clear,
In this woodland concert, all come near.

Songs from the Sundrenched Sky

High above, a flock of crows,
Wears sunglasses and shiny clothes.
They croon of tales with a twisty spin,
Of wind-blown hair and goofy grins.

A sunbeam bounces, giggles loud,
While clouds pass by, a fluffy crowd.
They moan in rhythm, a cottony sound,
As nature's jesters gather around.

The rain joins in, with a silly splash,
While puddles reflect a vibrant flash.
With melodies soaring, funny and bright,
We dance in delight 'neath the sunny light.

Ballads from the Berry Boughs

Underneath the berry boughs,
A frog sings loud, he takes his vows.
With berries bright, he forms a band,
A merry tune across the land.

A squirrel winks with berry stash,
While chipmunks dance, they make a splash.
The hedgehog joins, he's got some sass,
In a berry ballad, they all amass.

The sun dips down, the night comes near,
Their rhymes evolve, no room for fear.
With funny hats made from the leaves,
These silly songs, the garden grieves.

They laugh and play, till dawn's first light,
The berry boughs, a grand delight.
In every note, a joy bestowed,
A jolly choir on their leafy road.

The Symphony of Seasonal Shifts.

When winter's frost begins to creep,
The squirrels dance, they do not sleep.
They grip their nuts, a true ballet,
To find a friend, they sing and sway.

As spring arrives with sunny skies,
The bunnies prance, a grand surprise.
They trip and fall, then giggle loud,
A wobbly jig, they're quite the crowd.

Summer sings with bees on call,
The flowers bloom, they stand so tall.
With honey hats, the ants they cheer,
A bustling beat, it's crystal clear.

When autumn struts with colors bright,
The leaves drop tune, a funny sight.
The critters dance with windblown cheer,
A symphony where all is clear.

Whispers in the Garden

In the garden where secrets hide,
The rabbits plot, they're full of pride.
With carrots sharp, they make a list,
Of silly plans too good to miss.

The plants gossip, their tales unwind,
Of butterflies that intertwined.
A ladybug claims she's the best,
While worms just laugh, they take their rest.

The roses wink, their blooms so bright,
They play a game of hide and bite.
With colors wild and laughter free,
They whisper tales of revelry.

As twilight falls, the moon takes stage,
The garden laughs, its heart a page.
In every nook, a joke is spun,
In whispers shared, the night's such fun.

Stanzas in Bloom

In a field where flowers sway,
The bumblebees sing, "Hooray!"
With petals soft, they play around,
In every dance, pure joy is found.

The daisies giggle, their heads held high,
While butterflies flutter, catching sky.
They twirl in circles, what a scene,
This garden party, where all are keen.

The sun smiles down, a radiant beam,
As flowers share their zany dream.
In every color, a silly rhyme,
These stanzas bloom, the world in mime.

As dusk rolls in, the crickets play,
The flowers sigh, "What a day!"
With laughter bright, the night unfolds,
In stanzas shared, great fun retold.

www.ingramcontent.com/pod-product-compliance
Lightning Source LLC
Chambersburg PA
CBHW070751220426
43209CB00083B/448